MW01265588

THIS BOOK BELONGS TO

Made in the USA
Monee, IL
21 April 2025

16188629R00066